GOALS

Transforming Dreams into Daily Action

L E A P Learning Empowerment & Achieving Potential

ISBN 978-93-81115-67-1

First published in 2011 by Leadstart
A brand of One Point Six Technologies Private Limited
Unit no. 26, Ground Floor, A1, Shram Safalya,
Wadala Truck Terminal Road, Near Post Office,
Antop Hill, Mumbai -400037.
Email:info@leadstartcorp.com
www.leadstartcorp.com

Marketed & Distributed in India by Unbound Script
2/41, Ansari Road, Darayaganj, Delhi - 110002

EDITORS OF LEADSTART

The Editors of Leadstart are a team of passionate literary enthusiasts with a creative and progressive focus. Our team includes distinguished authors, researchers, contributors, in-house editors, and writing talent from around the world. Many literary projects require a diverse team rather than a single author to write or update the book. These projects often involve cases where the original author is unable to continue, whether because they are no longer available or have passed away. Our work thus spans a range of content, from original writings to thoughtfully abridged classics, updated editions, and translations.

ABOUT THE LEAP SERIES

The LEAP series of books has been conceived as a tool of empowerment for every individual to achieve their full potential.

There are certain aspirations that every person in the world shares. We all want to be happy. We all want to lead fulfilling lives. We all want to find our soulmate. We all want a job we love doing. We all want good friends who will share our joy and sorrow. We all want to believe that there is a purpose to our lives.

While the commonality of these goals spans the globe, their achievement is entirely individual. Each person possesses a unique and mixed gift of strengths and weaknesses, special talents and handicaps. To focus our individual lives on all that is positive within us, all that is possible for us to do, to be and to achieve, we need to take conscious steps towards it. The empowerment of our lives is an individual pursuit. The decisions are yours. The action is yours. To do the very best with what one has been given – that is the ultimate achievement of a life well lived.

You Are You
First, we must recognise ourselves and accept our particular basket of capabilities. Nobody is the same. Nor is it necessary to be like someone else.

Find Your Horizons
Once we are at peace with the composition of our own individuality, we can set out to enhance our capabilities in order to achieve full potential as an individual. We can utilise all the teaching around us to stretch our talents to the fullest extent to achieve worthwhile goals.

Cap The Leak
Once we recognise our potential, we can work to minimise the influence and impact of our weak points to allow the strengths to shine in everything we do.

Row Your Boat
Every day is part of the journey. Sometimes you win the day. Sometimes the day is lost. But you keep rowing towards the shore, towards your goals. In India, it is called sadhana. That special power within you drives you to achieve what you have set yourself to do.

The LEAP series teaches methods of individual empowerment.

ꟸ ꟹ

CONTENTS

INTRODUCTION
The Modern Landscape of Goals

In every generation, people have searched for progress, but never before has progress been so confusing. We live in a time of infinite choice and relentless movement, where information floods every waking hour and our attention feels constantly under siege. The modern world offers endless possibilities to learn, connect, and create. You can study from your living room, launch a business from your phone, and access more knowledge in a week than entire generations once could in a lifetime. Yet despite this abundance of opportunity, many people find themselves unsure where to begin, what to focus on, or why their work feels increasingly hollow. It is not opportunity that we lack, but direction.

In this restless environment, goals have never been more necessary. They bring structure to possibility and turn vague intention into tangible movement. A goal is not just an endpoint on a list; it is a declaration of purpose. It clarifies what matters and aligns your attention with your values. When your goals are anchored in something meaningful, effort no longer feels scattered. Work begins to carry a quiet satisfaction because each step, no matter how small, leads somewhere intentional.

In that sense, goals are not just about productivity; they are about coherence. They transform the chaos of a busy life into a sequence of deliberate actions.

Yet for many people, the word "goal" feels loaded. It has become tangled with pressure, perfectionism, and comparison. In school, we are told to set goals to succeed. In careers, we are asked to reach targets or milestones. On social media, we see others celebrating achievements that seem unreachable or unrealistic. This constant exposure can turn the process of self-improvement into a silent competition, where every step forward feels like it still isn't enough. Modern goal setting must be different. It must start not with external metrics but with internal alignment. The question is not only "What do I want to achieve?" but also "Why does this matter to me?" and "What kind of person do I want to become along the way?"

Purpose sits at the core of every sustainable goal. It is the emotional engine that drives persistence when motivation fades and the compass that helps you course-correct when circumstances change. Without purpose, goals become hollow checkboxes, easily abandoned when life grows difficult. But with purpose, even the smallest achievement carries meaning, because it becomes part of something larger. A student studying late at night, a professional learning a new skill, or a parent trying to balance work and family, all are sustained by a deeper reason that ties their effort to their identity. Purpose transforms goals from tasks into expressions of who we are and what we value.

This book was created for that reason: to help you reconnect with purpose, design goals that fit your life, and build the systems that make them real. Each chapter is structured to move from reflection to action. You will begin by understanding why goals matter and how they shape the way you think and feel. You will learn how to set meaningful objectives, plan them intelligently, and navigate the distractions and doubts that inevitably appear along the way. You will explore how motivation works in today's attention-driven world and how to recover when willpower runs low. Later chapters will guide you through collaboration, personal reflection, and tools to track your progress with honesty and self-compassion.

The goal of this book is not to turn you into a perfectly efficient person. It is to help you become more intentional. True productivity is not about doing more; it is about doing what matters with presence and understanding. You will see that success is not a single destination but an ongoing process of learning, adapting, and realigning your time with your values. Whether you are a student trying to find direction, a professional striving for balance, or someone seeking renewal after burnout, you will find here a framework that applies across stages of life.

Before you begin, pause for a moment to take stock of where you are. Think about what drives you and what you want to give shape to in the coming months or years. Ask yourself what success really means to you now, not what it used to mean or what it means to someone else. Write it down, even if the words feel uncertain. Your understanding begins in these small moments of honesty.

The chapters that follow are not meant to rush you but to guide you. They will remind you that progress is personal. The path to meaning is not measured by speed but by consistency and care.

You do not need to have everything figured out before you start. You simply need to begin. Every goal, no matter how large, begins with a single decision: to take the first small step with intention. From there, progress builds its own momentum. The rest of this journey will help you learn how to keep that momentum alive through clarity, balance, and purpose.

ꕥ

1

WHY GOALS MATTER

Every person carries an unstated sense that life can be shaped rather than merely endured, yet that sense only becomes real once it is harnessed by purpose. Purpose is the thread that ties days together and turns activity into progress, and when purpose is translated into a goal, it stops being an abstract concept in your head and becomes a direction you can follow. In a culture that invites you to react all day, goals function like a compass you choose rather than a tide you obey. They ask you to decide what deserves your attention, how you will spend your effort, and who you intend to become through that effort. Without this deliberate choice, you can move constantly and still feel that you have not moved at all. With it, the same hours gain shape and consequence, because you are no longer measuring your life by what you did, but by what those actions were for. Goals give structure to meaning. They translate values into choices, choices into habits, and habits into results you can stand behind.

Modern life multiplies the need for this structure. The volume of information, the velocity of change, and the availability of comparison can fracture attention and drain resolve long before you begin anything significant. When you do not know what you are moving toward, it becomes easy to surrender your day to the newest request or the loudest notification. Goals protect you from that drift by establishing a hierarchy of importance that is personal rather than accidental. They let you answer the two questions that govern achievement in any field: What matters most right now, and what matters most over time. Once those answers exist, tradeoffs become clearer and countless small decisions become simpler, because you are no longer deciding in a vacuum.

Setting a goal is not just a planning exercise. It is a statement about identity. When you commit to a target, you are saying that this outcome and the person capable of creating it belong to you. That is why the most effective goals are anchored in purpose and aligned with values; they feel like an extension of who you are rather than an external assignment. This alignment will not remove difficulty, but it will change your relationship to it. Friction still exists, deadlines still loom, and setbacks still occur, yet effort feels justified because it serves meaning rather than ego or expectation. Over time, this alignment reshapes self-trust. Each time you follow through, it becomes evidence that you live in agreement with yourself, and evidence is the strongest foundation for confidence.

Achievement, however, is not the only reason goals matter. The pursuit itself is formative. Working toward a clear objective forces you to refine judgment, expand skills, and manage emotion. You learn how to start when you feel unready, how to continue when novelty fades, and how to revise when conditions change. These are transferable capacities that improve every area of life, from study and work to relationships and health. The project may end, but the person you became while pursuing it remains. This is why even unrealised goals can hold value when you use them as instruments for growth. Progress measured only by outcomes will always feel fragile. Progress measured by the capabilities you build along the way becomes durable.

The absence of goals carries its own cost. Without direction, your decisions will not coherently accumulate, and days pass without narrative. You feel the weight of unfinished intentions, but cannot name them clearly enough to act. That condition breeds restlessness and doubt, because human beings are not satisfied by motion alone; we are satisfied by meaningful motion. People often describe this unsettled state as a lack of motivation, but more often it is a lack of clarity. Once the destination is defined, the mind can organise itself around it. Attention narrows, distractions lose appeal, and the same energy that felt scattered becomes concentrated. Clarity does not eliminate resistance, yet it lowers the friction of beginning and returning.

Contemporary realities make this conversation broader than career achievement or academic milestones. Students navigate hybrid learning and algorithmic distraction while trying to choose a path that may shift with the economy. Professionals balance remote work, global collaboration, and rapid reskilling in industries that reinvent themselves every few years. Caregivers design days around responsibilities that rarely fit tidy schedules. Creators and founders move through cycles of uncertainty that can magnify self-doubt. Across these contexts, goals offer the same stabilising function. They help you decide what to learn next, what to protect on your calendar, what to decline gracefully, and what to start even when your nerves insist on waiting.

Meaningful goals begin with a why that can withstand fatigue and delay. The why does not have to be grand to be powerful; it just has to be honest. Perhaps you want to finish a degree because education represents freedom in your family. Perhaps you want to improve your health because you wish to be present for your child's milestones. Perhaps you want to master a skill because craftsmanship brings you alive. When the reason is real, discipline becomes an expression of care rather than punishment. The same task that once felt like a burden begins to feel like a vote for a life you chose. This shift is subtle on the surface and profound beneath it, because it transforms effort from something you endure into something you invest.

None of this implies that goals must be rigid. Life changes, and wise plans change with it. The purpose of a goal is guidance, not confinement. You can adjust timelines without abandoning intentions, revise metrics without diluting meaning, and replace a path that no longer fits with one that does. Flexibility protects commitment by keeping it compatible with reality. The most resilient individuals hold the destination firmly and the route loosely. They review progress, learn from feedback, and repeat without shame, because revising yourself is not a confession of failure. It is how you attain mastery.

If you struggle to begin, start at the end. Picture the result with as much concrete detail as possible: the exam submitted, the portfolio shipped, the first month of savings completed, the performance delivered with steadiness rather than fear. Then work backwards to identify the few actions that would make this picture more likely. Break those actions into beginnings small enough to do today, and do one. Vision without action is a wish. Action without vision is a grind. The pairing of both creates a sustainable rhythm because it tells you not only what to do, but why doing it matters now.

Finally, remember that goals are not solely about personal gain. The most satisfying aims often include contribution, whether that means teaching what you have learned, mentoring someone a few steps behind, or shaping work that improves a corner of the world you can actually touch. Contribution enlarges purpose, and an enlarged purpose tends to enlarge perseverance. When your progress lifts others, your own motivation deepens, because the work stands for more than your advancement.

Goals matter because they turn time into a story you have authored. They allow you to live life by your own design rather than by default, to measure success not only by what you reach, but by who you become through the reaching. For now, let this first decision be simple and specific: choose one aim that deserves your attention, give it a true reason, and take the smallest step that proves you have begun.

ഊര

2

SETTING GOALS WITH PURPOSE

Every goal begins as a thought, an awareness that something in your life could be shaped more deliberately. It might emerge as ambition, curiosity, or even discontent. Perhaps you want to learn a new skill, change careers, or create more balance in your day. These ideas often start small and shaky, but within them lies the potential for transformation. Yet, not every impulse deserves to grow into a goal. The difference between a fleeting thought and a life-changing pursuit lies in purpose. Purpose gives your goal depth and durability. It connects effort to meaning and turns the daily discipline of work into something coherent and satisfying. Without purpose, even the most organised plan can feel hollow, and the accomplishment at the end can feel strangely empty. With it, every step, no matter how small, begins to feel like a step toward a life that makes sense.

To set goals with purpose, you must first distinguish between what you *think* you want and what you truly desire. This distinction sounds simple, but it is often blurred by the noise of other people's expectations. Many people chase goals handed down by family, culture, or social comparison, achievements that sound impressive but do not resonate internally. This is why you might meet every external marker of success and still feel disconnected from yourself. The goal existed, but it was never *yours*. Purposeful goals begin from reflection and life experiences. They come from pausing long enough to ask: "What do I want because it feels meaningful to me, not because it will look good to others?" Sitting with that question is not easy; it requires honesty and patience. But that's when the real answers begin to take shape.

When you start to define what truly matters, goals become tools of transformation rather than tests of worth. They become the bridge between who you are now and who you are capable of becoming. Yet meaning alone does not build momentum. A purpose must be matched with structure, clarity, and realism, or else it remains a pleasant idea that never turns into action. Clarity is what transforms a dream into a plan. It turns "I want to get fit" into "I will walk thirty minutes every morning before work." It turns "I want to be financially stable" into "I will set aside ten per cent of my income each month." These definitions matter because they give the mind something tangible to pursue. The more precise your goal, the more measurable your progress becomes, and the easier it is to build consistency.

Short-Term and Long-Term Goals: Building a Ladder of Purpose

Every meaningful achievement is composed of many smaller victories. Long-term goals give you direction, but short-term goals give you traction. Both are essential. Long-term goals are the vision, broad, inspiring, and often stretching years into the future. Short-term goals are the stepping stones that make that vision possible, the actions that fill the space between aspiration and accomplishment. When you neglect one side of this relationship, your balance is lost. Too much focus on long-term dreams and you drift into abstraction; too much focus on short-term tasks and you risk busyness without meaning.

A practical way to combine both is to treat goal setting as a ladder: each rung represents progress. For instance, if your long-term goal is to become a skilled musician, your short-term goals might involve learning scales, mastering rhythm, and performing small recitals. Each small milestone confirms capability and builds confidence for the next step. The ladder metaphor reminds you that achievement is cumulative; it grows through practice, patience, and steady repetition.

Goal Type	**Purpose**	**Example**	**Time Frame**
Long-Term	Defines overall direction	Build a creative business	3–5 years
Mid-Term	Connects big goals to actionable plans	Enrol in a design course, build a portfolio	6–12 months
Short-Term	Generates steady progress	Work on 2 projects a month	Weekly / Monthly

Use this table as a loose framework rather than a rigid formula. The aim is not to predict your entire future but to cultivate a sense of progression. Each tier should feel achievable but still challenge you to grow. Review them regularly. Life is fluid, and your priorities will shift as you do. A once urgent goal may lose its significance; another might quietly become central. Purposeful planning allows flexibility without losing direction. Think of it as sailing. You keep adjusting your sails, but the destination remains the same.

The **SMART** framework is a simple but profound way to turn ideas into action:

- **Specific:** Define exactly what you're doing. "Finish reading Chapter 4 of my marketing textbook" beats "Study."
- **Measurable:** Know when success is reached. "Finish a 10-slide presentation draft" gives you closure.
- **Achievable:** Match ambition with realism. Goals should challenge, not crush. "Run three times this week for 30 minutes" is far more realistic as a beginner than "running a marathon".
- **Relevant:** Ensure alignment with what truly matters to you. A goal that excites you sustains focus. "Study consumer trends to support my marketing project" aligns with your coursework, whereas "Browse general business news" spreads your energy too thin.
- **Time-bound:** Create urgency with a clear boundary. Without it, time expands indefinitely. "Complete my project proposal by Friday, 6 p.m." keeps momentum alive, without a time frame, time expands indefinitely.

But SMART goals are only the surface. What truly drives action is *emotional clarity*. Ask yourself: *Why does this goal matter to me?* When meaning is missing, motivation fades. Link each goal to a value: growth, freedom, contribution, mastery. That connection turns discipline into devotion.

Balancing Ambition with Realism

Ambition is the spark that moves you to dream bigger, but realism is the discipline that turns those dreams into results. A goal set too high can discourage progress before it begins, while one set too low can leave you uninspired. The art of balance lies in finding goals that feel slightly beyond reach, just enough to stretch you without breaking your spirit. This zone of productive discomfort is where growth happens.

For example, imagine a student who decides to complete a language course in three weeks, though the curriculum is designed for three months. The initial burst of excitement may carry her through a few days, but fatigue and frustration will soon follow. A better approach might be to aim for steady progress: one lesson every day, paired with ten minutes of conversation practice. This pace may seem slower, but it is sustainable, and sustainability is what produces mastery.

This principle applies equally to professionals. You might want to double your income or launch a new business, but without a timeline grounded in current resources, those goals can quickly become overwhelming. A better strategy is to scale down to what can be managed within your current reality, while still maintaining a long-term vision. Success built gradually has stronger roots than success forced prematurely.

When planning, remember that progress requires recovery. Periods of rest and renewal are not indulgences; they are strategic necessities. No goal can thrive in exhaustion. Schedule moments of review, reflection, and pause. Ask yourself: "Is this pace sustainable? Is this path still aligned with my purpose?" This rhythm of review ensures that ambition remains grounded in awareness.

How to Anchor Goals in Purpose

Purpose might seem abstract, but you can translate it into concrete practice through structured reflection. Each goal you set should be filtered through questions that keep it honest and personal.

1. **Define your "why."** Write down why this goal matters to you. Go deeper than the first answer. If your goal is to run a marathon, ask yourself why. Maybe it's about health, discipline, or proving resilience. Ask why each of those reasons matters until you reach the core motive that feels emotionally significant. That is your true source of energy.
2. **Connect it to your values.** Values act as the compass that ensures your goals point in the right direction. If you value creativity, design goals that allow for exploration. If you value family, ensure your goals don't consistently take you away from what matters most. Alignment between goals and values ensures peace, and not just progress.
3. **Envision the result.** Close your eyes and imagine what success feels like. Visualise the sights, sounds, and emotions of that moment. The clearer your vision, the stronger your belief. The brain responds to imagined success much like it does to real success; it rehearses victory and builds confidence.
4. **Map your process.** Every destination needs a route. Break the goal into actionable steps, then arrange those steps in logical

order. If the sequence feels overwhelming, start with one step that you can complete today.

5. **Prepare for resistance.** Every goal encounters opposition, distractions, fear, fatigue, or self-doubt. Anticipate them in advance and decide how you'll respond. For instance, if motivation dips, you might switch to shorter work intervals or find an accountability partner.

These steps don't just help you plan better; they protect your purpose from erosion. The more deliberate your preparation, the easier it becomes to persist when the excitement fades.

Avoiding Common Goal Traps

Even the most determined individuals fall into predictable traps that sap focus and confidence. Awareness of these patterns can help you steer clear of them.

1. **The Comparison Trap.** Measuring your progress against others will distort your sense of achievement. Growth is personal. The only fair comparison is between who you were and who you are becoming.
2. **The Perfection Trap.** Waiting for perfect timing or perfect skill is a form of delay disguised as preparation. Start where you are, and improve as you go.
3. **The Distraction Trap.** Spreading yourself across too many goals divides energy. Choose a few that matter deeply, and give them your best attention. Consistency in a few areas outperforms scattered effort across many.
4. **The Outcome Trap.** Focusing only on the result leads to frustration when progress feels slow. Instead, pay attention to the process,

the habits, systems, and mindset you are building. The person you become will outlast any single result.

Each of these traps stems from the same root problem: misaligned focus. When your attention shifts away from purpose, pressure replaces passion. The antidote is to return often to your why, your values, and your chosen path.

An Example in Practice

Consider a young teacher who decides she wants to "be more successful." At first, the goal sounds ambitious but vague. Through reflection, she redefines success: "I want to create lessons that engage students and build their curiosity." Now her goal expresses a clear purpose, impact, not image. For that purpose, actionable steps emerge: designing creative projects, seeking mentorship, and learning new teaching methods. Over time, her classroom changes, her confidence deepens, and success begins to feel meaningful.

The same principle applies universally. A student might shift focus from "getting good grades" to "understanding subjects well enough to use them creatively." A professional might replace "earning a promotion" with "developing skills that empower my team." When you pursue growth from a place of meaning, outcomes tend to follow naturally. Purpose refines direction; direction sustains motivation.

Reflection: A Framework for Alignment

Use the following framework to test the depth and honesty of your goals. It works for students, professionals, and anyone trying to bring clarity to their ambitions.

Question	Reflection Prompt
What do I truly want to achieve in the next year?	Write freely without censoring yourself. Honesty matters more than precision.
Why is this goal important to me?	Keep asking "why" until you reach an emotional truth.
Does this goal express one of my deepest values?	Identify the value: growth, love, stability, service, creativity, that it fulfils.
What will success look and feel like?	Describe specific, sensory details of that outcome.
What habits or support will I need?	Identify people, resources, and routines that can help.
How will I measure progress?	Choose milestones that reveal direction, not just completion.
What could derail me, and how will I respond?	Anticipate your obstacles and prepare strategies now.

Keep this framework nearby and revisit it whenever your motivation wavers. A goal that passes these questions becomes more than a plan; it becomes a reflection of who you are and where you are headed.

From Planning to Commitment

Once clarity is in place, the next step is to embody commitment. The hardest part of any journey is not the beginning but the middle, when initial enthusiasm fades and effort turns into routine. True commitment is not a burst of excitement but a quiet promise you renew daily. It is showing up for yourself even when no one is watching.

Consistency may feel unremarkable, but it is the most powerful force in self-development. Each repeated action lays another brick in the foundation of your identity. Over time, these bricks form confidence, resilience, and integrity, the very traits that sustain achievement. Commitment transforms intention into reality, and reality into habit.

When you set goals with purpose, you stop working to prove something and start working to express something. That shift changes everything. It gives you the patience to endure difficulty, the humility to learn, and the resilience to begin again after failure. It turns life from a checklist into a journey of deliberate creation.

A purposeful goal does not just change what you achieve. It changes how you live while achieving it.

ഇഗ

3

PLANNING AND PREPARING

Planning is the architecture of success. To plan is to translate dreams into structure, to give your intentions shape and sequence. Without planning, goals remain distant abstractions, floating like ideas without anchors. But when you begin to plan deliberately, you give those ideas gravity. You decide how time will be used, where effort will go, and how to move steadily from vision to reality. In this way, planning is not about controlling the future but about preparing yourself to meet it with purpose and awareness.

The essence of effective planning lies in balance: between imagination and realism, between long-term vision and immediate action. Too much dreaming without design leaves you idle; too much structure without imagination turns life mechanical. True planning sits in between; it listens to your hopes and translates them into movement. It asks: "If this is where I want to go, what must I do next? What can I do now?" This is how dreams are domesticated into days.

The most powerful plans begin with clarity. Clarity does not require that you know every step in advance; it only requires that you know your destination well enough to recognise progress when it happens. To reach that level of precision, write your goals down. The act of writing turns the abstract into something visible and accountable. It is a form of self-commitment, a contract with your future self. Even a single sentence can change how you act. "I will graduate in two years," or "I will save for six months before I start my business." Once written, such sentences stop being wishes and begin to feel like agreements you have promised to honour.

Yet, writing a plan is not merely about scheduling tasks. It is about aligning actions with values, designing days around meaning. Begin by mapping what truly matters to you: the priorities that define your sense of progress. Imagine your week as a container with limited space. Each action you plan to take occupies part of that space, so fill it intentionally. If your health matters, carve time for rest and nourishment. If relationships matter, make space for connection. Planning is not the pursuit of more but the art of choosing better. It is less about cramming every minute and more about curating what belongs within it.

A well-made plan also accepts change. Life rarely follows a straight line, and rigid plans often collapse under pressure. The most resilient planning systems allow for flexibility. They are frameworks rather than prisons. This means building schedules with open pockets of time for unexpected turns, interruptions, delays, and new opportunities. Think of your plan as a map drawn in pencil, ready to be redrawn when conditions shift. The habit of review is crucial here. Set aside a few minutes at the end of each day or week to reflect: What worked well? What didn't? What needs adjustment? These quiet reviews transform planning from a one-time act into a living process. They teach you how to adapt without losing focus.

To illustrate, imagine a student preparing for final exams. She lists the subjects, estimates the time required, and blocks out study sessions through the month. But she also includes margins, half-hours to revisit difficult topics, days left open for rest or unforeseen events. This provides structure without making your life too mechanical, leaving you space to breathe and keeping you efficient. The same principle applies in every sphere, whether you are managing a business, developing a project, or pursuing personal growth. The goal is not to script your life minute by minute but to give it rhythm and intention.

Good planning is inseparable from preparation. Preparation is how you make tomorrow easier before it arrives. It is the act of removing friction before action begins. A prepared person does not simply have a plan written down; they have thought through the materials, the environment, and the mindset needed to execute it. A writer prepares by outlining ideas and setting up their workspace. A student prepares by organising notes the night before. A leader prepares by anticipating questions, studying context, and clarifying decisions before meetings begin. In every case, preparation is what transforms anxiety into confidence. It ensures that when the time for action comes, you are not distracted by avoidable confusion.

Preparation also means emotional readiness. Many plans fail not because they were flawed, but because the person following them lost heart midway. You cannot plan effectively if you ignore your energy. Ask yourself what helps you feel grounded and what drains you. Build your days around energy rhythms, moments of high focus and periods of rest. In the morning, you might handle your most demanding work; in the afternoon, tasks that require less creativity but more consistency. Learn to plan for your mind, not against it. In doing so, you move from forcing discipline to designing for it.

Another aspect of preparation is anticipating obstacles before they appear. This is not pessimism but strategic foresight. Before beginning a project or a goal, list the potential disruptions: unexpected costs, competing priorities, and loss of motivation. Then, think of countermeasures, ways to mitigate or respond when those obstacles arise. For instance, if you know fatigue is a recurring barrier, build a rest day into your weekly structure. If procrastination is your weakness, set external accountability: a mentor, a progress tracker, or even a daily reminder system. Preparation is simply foresight in action, a way of saying, "I know challenges will come, but I will not meet them unprepared."

In the modern world, planning has acquired new dimensions. With digital calendars, productivity tools, and countless time-management philosophies, it can be tempting to confuse organisation with effectiveness. But no technology can substitute for clarity of intent. Use systems as supports, not as substitutes for thought. Experiment with digital planners, habit trackers, or traditional notebooks if they help you stay consistent. The right system is the one that encourages calm rather than clutter. The danger of modern productivity culture is that it often glorifies busyness over progress. Real planning should feel grounded, not frantic. If your system exhausts you, simplify it.

One of the most overlooked parts of planning is reflection, the pause between action and adjustment. Many people execute plans relentlessly without stopping to evaluate whether their direction still makes sense. This is how burnout occurs: the mind continues to run long after meaning has left. A sustainable plan includes built-in reflection points. Weekly reflections can ask simple questions: What brought me closer to my purpose this week? What can I do differently next week? What needs to be paused or removed? These questions help convert experience into wisdom. Reflection makes your plan a teacher rather than a task list.

Planning is also a dialogue with time. It teaches you to treat time as a partner rather than an enemy. Many people see time as something to fight or control, but time is neither opponent nor ally; it is simply the medium through which life unfolds. When you plan wisely, you learn to live with time instead of against it. You stop racing through your days and begin moving through them with presence. The more consciously you design your days, the less they slip away unnoticed.

It is worth remembering that even the best plans are only sketches of possibilities. The plan itself is not the achievement; it is the pattern that allows achievement to occur. The painter must still pick up the brush, the student must still open the book, the professional must still take the meeting. The purpose of a plan is to remove excuses, not to replace action. Each morning, the plan is an invitation to begin again.

True planning does not create rigidity; it creates freedom, the freedom that comes from knowing what matters and from having prepared enough to pursue it without panic. When your plans are built on purpose, balanced with realism, and executed with awareness, they stop feeling like obligations. They start feeling like direction itself.

So begin your planning not as a chore but as a conversation with your future. Ask what version of yourself you wish to meet a year from now, and let your plan be the bridge to that encounter. Write down what matters. Anticipate what might falter. Prepare your environment, your mind, and your heart. Then begin, not with haste but with quiet assurance, knowing that you have already met half the journey through preparation alone.

ꕥ

4

MOTIVATION AND WILLPOWER

Motivation is often imagined as a burst of energy, a surge of enthusiasm that sweeps away hesitation and launches us into action. Yet anyone who has tried to build something lasting knows that this initial spark rarely lasts long. Real progress is not driven by these moments of inspiration but by what happens after they fade. Motivation begins a journey, but willpower carries it through. The two together form a rhythm: one provides direction, the other endurance. Without both, even the best plans can lose momentum and drift into delay.

True motivation grows from meaning, not mood. People often wait to "feel ready," believing that once the right moment comes, they will finally begin. But readiness does not precede action; it follows it. Motivation strengthens in motion. When you take even a small step toward something important, you create proof that your actions have power. The mind responds to that evidence by producing more energy to continue. This is why progress, no matter how small, is so critical. It builds a feedback loop between action and belief. Once you begin, you find that what felt impossible starts to look manageable. What seemed distant starts to come within reach.

But meaning is the deeper current that keeps this cycle alive. When you care about what you are doing for reasons that reach beyond convenience or approval, your motivation becomes resilient. A student who studies only to meet deadlines will tire quickly, but one who studies to master ideas that inspire them will persist through difficulty. A professional who works only for reward may lose energy when recognition is delayed, while one who works to create, to serve, or to contribute continues even in quiet stretches. When your motivation is rooted in purpose, you stop needing to be pushed from the outside. The work itself becomes self-renewing.

Even so, there are days when meaning feels distant. Fatigue, disappointment, and distraction can erode focus. This is where willpower takes over. Willpower is not a burst of intensity; it is steady, deliberate control over attention and effort. It allows you to stay aligned with your values when your feelings pull you away. Psychologists describe willpower as a limited resource, one that can be depleted by constant decision-making or by resisting temptation over time. This is why structure matters so much. The more predictable your routines, the fewer choices you must make under pressure, and the more energy remains for true challenges.

Imagine two people trying to follow a healthy lifestyle. The first decides each morning whether to exercise or rest, what to eat, and when to start work. The second has a plan already in place: exercise before breakfast, meal prep done on Sunday, and work starts at nine.

The second person's willpower lasts longer because fewer decisions are left to impulse. Structure transforms willpower from a daily struggle into a supportive framework. It prevents the fatigue that comes from constant choice.

Another truth about willpower is that it thrives on kindness, not punishment. Many people treat discipline as an act of aggression against their own laziness. They force themselves to work, criticise themselves for weakness, and confuse self-control with self-denial. But lasting willpower grows from cooperation, not conflict. If you constantly fight with yourself, you eventually lose. The key is to design your environment and schedule in ways that make the right actions easier and the wrong ones less tempting. If you want to read more, keep a book visible on your desk. If you want to avoid distractions, move your phone out of reach. Each of these adjustments supports your effort without requiring constant struggle.

Motivation also depends on rhythm. The mind cannot maintain high intensity endlessly. It needs alternating cycles of focus and recovery. Trying to push without pause leads to exhaustion, and exhaustion leads to apathy. To protect motivation, build periods of renewal into your day. Rest is not the absence of effort; it is what allows effort to continue. Short walks, moments of silence, a stretch between tasks, these are not indulgences but essential tools of sustainability. The goal is not to work harder but to work with greater awareness of your natural energy cycles.

Progress is easier to maintain when it can be seen. The brain is motivated by visible evidence of success, however small. This is why checklists, trackers, and journals are more than organisational tools;

they are psychological reinforcements. Each completed task releases a small satisfaction that reinforces your confidence to continue. Keep a record of what you have done, not only what remains undone. This changes the emotional tone of effort from scarcity to growth. Instead of focusing on what is missing, you begin to see what is possible.

Still, every plan will face moments of resistance. There will be days when enthusiasm feels completely out of reach. On such days, the smallest act matters most. Begin with the smallest version of the task you are avoiding. Write one sentence, solve one problem, tidy one corner. Once movement begins, inertia breaks. You will often find that the energy you were waiting for appears only after you start. Action generates energy; waiting consumes it. The courage to start small is what separates the disciplined from the defeated.

Habits are the quiet machinery behind motivation. They are the systems that carry effort forward when emotion wavers. A habit turns repeated action into instinct. The first time you sit to work early, it feels like a decision. After a month, it feels like who you are. The beauty of habits is that they convert willpower into autopilot. What once required conscious effort becomes automatic, freeing your mind for higher challenges. Building a habit begins with consistency, not volume. Choose a manageable routine and repeat it until it no longer feels negotiable. That stability will carry you through the rough days when enthusiasm falters.

Community also plays a hidden role in sustaining motivation. Humans are social learners, and the behaviour of those around us quietly shapes our own. Surround yourself with people who value focus and growth. Their presence creates a climate where perseverance feels natural. This doesn't mean imitation; it means inspiration. Seeing others commit to their work, recover from setbacks, or approach their goals with calm determination reminds you that persistence is possible. Conversation itself can renew your energy. Sometimes encouragement from another person can reconnect you to your own reasons for starting.

Perhaps the most misunderstood part of motivation is its relationship with failure. Many people interpret setbacks as proof that they lack discipline, when in truth, failure is part of every long effort. Each lapse, delay, or wrong turn provides information about what works, what doesn't, and where your current systems need refinement. The right response to failure is not guilt but curiosity. Ask yourself, "What can I learn from this?" Every honest answer strengthens your understanding of how you operate. Willpower becomes wiser when it learns from fatigue rather than denying it.

Motivation also thrives in emotional connection. Anchoring your effort to something symbolic, a photograph, a sentence written on your wall, or a promise to someone you care about, gives your work an added dimension of purpose. These symbols remind you that what you are doing reaches beyond daily struggle. A note to your future self, for instance, can become a source of strength on difficult days. It is a quiet reminder that your present discipline is a gift to your future peace.

Over time, motivation and willpower blend into something deeper: trust in yourself. Each time you begin without waiting for perfect conditions, each time you complete something you promised to finish, you prove that your actions can be relied upon. This quiet reliability builds confidence that cannot be faked. You begin to act not out of pressure, but from integrity. You follow through because you trust yourself to do so. That self-trust becomes the ultimate fuel, steadier than enthusiasm, more durable than excitement.

Motivation is not a light that flickers on and off. It is a fire that must be tended. Some days, it burns bright and effortlessly. Other days, it dims and must be fed by small, deliberate actions, a well-timed rest, a supportive conversation, a few minutes of reflection. If you learn how to keep that fire alive without waiting for inspiration to strike, you will discover a form of strength that lasts far beyond any single success. Willpower then stops being a struggle and becomes a quiet partnership between who you are and who you wish to become.

In the end, the question is not how to stay motivated forever, but how to return to motivation whenever it fades. If you can build that skill, the ability to begin again, patiently and without despair, then you will never truly lose momentum. You will learn that progress does not depend on constant excitement but on the steady willingness to continue. And that is the essence of mastery: to do what matters, again and again, until effort itself becomes ease.

ഌ ര

5

OVERCOMING OBSTACLES

Every path of growth is met with resistance. It is a natural law of human progress that the moment you set a clear intention, the world seems to rise to test it. Challenges appear not as coincidences, but as mirrors, reflecting both your strengths and your unpreparedness. They stretch the will and expose the gaps between desire and discipline, between imagination and effort. Yet it is precisely within these gaps that true development occurs. Obstacles are not barriers meant to stop you; they are thresholds through which understanding deepens and endurance forms. Without resistance, there can be no resilience. Without difficulty, there can be no depth. The person who glides easily through every situation learns little about patience, adaptability, or creative problem-solving. The person who struggles, stumbles, reflects, and begins again develops an inner strength that cannot be taught by comfort.

When we first meet resistance, our instinct is often to turn away. Frustration, fatigue, and doubt surface, whispering that perhaps we were mistaken to try. These emotions are not evidence of weakness; they are natural responses to uncertainty. But when we stop at the first feeling of discomfort, we mistake friction for failure. What is really being asked of us in such moments is attention. Every obstacle carries a message about the current limits of our ability or understanding. If we pause long enough to listen, we begin to see patterns: perhaps our planning was too rigid, our expectations too high, our energy misdirected, or our motivation tethered to shallow rewards. The obstacle becomes a teacher, not a punishment. In this sense, every difficulty contains a piece of wisdom, but only those willing to face it with patience can uncover it.

Most of life's obstacles are not external events but internal conditions. Fear, procrastination, indecision, and self-doubt are barriers far more stubborn than circumstance. They arise quietly, disguised as logic or caution, convincing us that it is better to wait, to delay, to gather more certainty before we act. But no amount of waiting will erase fear; it will only deepen its hold. The courage to act while uncertain, to take the first imperfect step despite resistance, is what dismantles fear's power. Each time we confront hesitation with movement, we reinforce a new identity, one built on trust rather than avoidance. That trust grows slowly, through small acts of persistence, until it becomes a kind of faith in ourselves. It tells us that while we cannot control what happens around us, we can always control our willingness to continue.

External obstacles, on the other hand, often force us to face reality. They strip away illusion and ask us to see our situation clearly. Financial strain, limited opportunities, or unexpected responsibilities can feel like walls closing in. Yet even within those walls, there is room to think, to plan, to adapt. When resources are few, creativity expands. When time is short, priorities sharpen. Constraints, rather than crushing potential, can refine it. Many of the world's most enduring achievements were born not from abundance, but from necessity, from people who had to find new ways to do old things because the familiar paths were no longer open. The challenge, then, is not only to overcome obstacles, but to learn to work with them, to turn resistance into raw material for growth.

The most resilient individuals are not those who face fewer problems but those who interpret their problems differently. They have trained themselves to view obstacles not as verdicts but as feedback. When a plan fails, they ask what it reveals about their methods or mindset. When a door closes, they look for another or build their own. This adaptive intelligence is what distinguishes resilience from stubbornness. Stubbornness insists on one path, one outcome, one way of winning. Resilience, in contrast, accepts change, bends without breaking, and discovers new routes toward the same destination. Life, like water, always finds a way forward. And those who learn to move like water, patient, flexible, persistent, are rarely defeated for long.

It is often said that failure builds character, but that phrase simplifies what is actually a complex psychological process. Failure does not automatically strengthen us; it only does so when we are willing to face it honestly. Many people respond to failure with denial or self-blame, refusing to learn from it. But those who examine it carefully, who extract its lessons without letting it define their worth, experience something transformative. They realise that the experience of failure is not a commentary on their identity, but simply a mirror reflecting what must still be refined. They begin to separate self-worth from success, understanding that both are part of the same continuum of effort and evolution. This realisation frees them from perfectionism and makes them more daring, because the fear of falling no longer paralyses them.

In every enduring success story lies an extended history of obstacles faced, lessons learned, and directions changed. It is easy to admire the outcome but overlook the discipline it took to persist through disappointment, fatigue, and discouragement. What makes persistence possible is not blind determination but renewed perspective. When the original motivation fades, when progress slows, the wise learn to pause and remember their purpose. They reconnect to the deeper "why" beneath the goal, the value, belief, or principle that gives it meaning. This reconnection replenishes emotional energy. Purpose is the antidote to despair, because it restores a sense of direction even when the path is uncertain.

Sometimes the wisest response to an obstacle is not to push harder, but to step back and recover. Fatigue can cloud judgment just as effectively as fear. Rest, reflection, and renewal are not signs of surrender but strategies of endurance. Many breakthroughs come not from relentless effort but from stillness, from moments when the mind, freed from strain, suddenly sees clearly. A balanced rhythm between effort and rest prevents burnout and keeps your purpose alive. The goal is not constant motion but sustainable motion, progress that endures rather than progress that consumes.

Another essential aspect of overcoming obstacles is community. Human beings are not designed to endure life's challenges in isolation. Sharing struggles, seeking perspective, or simply being witnessed in moments of difficulty can lighten emotional weight and reveal solutions that solitude obscures. Support does not diminish independence; it strengthens it by restoring balance. Every person who achieves something meaningful has, in some way, drawn upon the insight, patience, or kindness of others. It is a form of wisdom to accept help without shame and to offer it without superiority. Obstacles remind us that resilience is not only an individual capacity but a collective one.

Stress, which often accompanies difficulty, is not inherently destructive. It becomes harmful only when it remains unmanaged. Properly understood, stress is a signal that something in our system, physical, emotional, or mental, needs attention. It can even serve as a form of guidance, pointing us toward imbalance or unmet needs. The key lies in listening rather than reacting. Instead of suppressing stress, acknowledge it and trace its source. Is it rooted in fear, overcommitment, lack of clarity, or fatigue? Awareness allows for adjustment. The same force that overwhelms one person can motivate another, depending on how it is interpreted. Managing stress, therefore, begins not with control, but with comprehension.

The final and perhaps most profound lesson in overcoming obstacles is that they are not interruptions to your journey; they *are* the journey. Without them, growth would be theoretical. With them, growth becomes a lived experience. Every time you meet resistance with patience, every time you fail and begin again, you redefine who you are. You shift from seeking an easy path to seeking a meaningful one. The reward of such a path is not the absence of hardship, but the quiet confidence that you can face it without losing yourself. The more you practice this, the more unshakable your calm becomes.

Overcoming obstacles is not about triumph in the traditional sense. It is about endurance with awareness, progress with humility, and adaptation with grace. When you stop seeing challenges as proof that something has gone wrong and start seeing them as invitations to refine your character, life itself becomes a form of practice. Each obstacle, once passed through, adds texture and wisdom to your days. The road is never meant to be smooth; it is meant to reveal the strength of your stride.

And in time, you may even come to welcome the tests that once frightened you. For you will have learned that every barrier overcome deepens your understanding, and every detour taken opens new territory of the self. What once seemed like resistance becomes rhythm, the natural pulse of a life moving forward, learning, falling, and rising again, with ever-growing steadiness and light.

ꕤ

6

UNDERSTANDING YOURSELF

Every journey toward achievement begins with a return inward. Before you can shape the world, you must first understand the one that exists within you. Without this understanding, goals lose coherence; they become scattered, driven by imitation or impulse rather than truth. To understand yourself is to uncover the quiet patterns beneath your choices, the desires that guide you, the fears that limit you, and the values that make you feel most alive. This understanding does not arise in a single moment of revelation; it grows through reflection, experience, and honesty. The work is subtle but essential, because self-knowledge is the compass that keeps every other form of progress aligned. Without it, even great effort can lead you astray.

The first step in understanding yourself is learning to listen. The world is filled with noise, opinions, expectations, and advice that compete for your attention. Much of it is well-intentioned, yet if absorbed unfiltered, it drowns out your own voice. To know yourself, you must create moments of silence, spaces where you can hear the faint but unmistakable rhythm of your own thoughts. In those quiet intervals, you begin to distinguish what is truly yours from what you have simply inherited from others. Ask yourself not only what you want, but *why* you want it. Is your goal a reflection of personal conviction or an attempt to meet someone else's standard of success? The difference may seem small, but over time, it determines the shape of your entire life. A borrowed goal drains energy; a genuine one replenishes it.

Self-understanding deepens when you begin to observe yourself as both actor and witness. This dual awareness allows you to see your life not just from within your habits, but from beyond them. You notice the moments when your reactions are automatic, the places where emotion overrides reason, or where self-doubt quiets your initiative. Instead of judging these patterns, study them. They are not flaws to hide, but data to learn from. For example, if you tend to delay difficult tasks, ask what emotion sits beneath the delay. Is it fear of failure, fatigue, or lack of clarity? If you find yourself drawn to certain kinds of people or work, ask what values those affinities reflect. Every behaviour carries a story, and when you begin to read those stories carefully, your choices start to make sense. Understanding yourself is, in many ways, an act of gentle curiosity.

True self-awareness also involves acknowledging contradictions. Human beings are not simple; we contain many selves, each shaped by circumstance and time. You may be both ambitious and afraid, confident and uncertain, generous and self-protective. To deny these contradictions is to split yourself in two. To accept them is to become whole. The aim of self-knowledge is not to simplify who you are, but to integrate your complexity into coherence. When you allow all parts of yourself a seat at the table, the disciplined, the impulsive, the idealistic, the pragmatic, you discover balance. Growth then becomes less about erasing what you dislike and more about harmonising the forces within you so that they move in the same direction.

Another key part of understanding yourself lies in recognising your values, the principles that give shape to your decisions. Values act as the internal architecture of purpose. They determine what feels right and what does not, what you pursue and what you resist. Without clarity about your values, you may find yourself achieving things that do not bring satisfaction, wondering why success feels hollow. Reflect on the moments when you have felt most alive or at peace. What was present in those experiences? Integrity, creativity, connection, freedom, learning, kindness? These are clues to your personal hierarchy of meaning. Once identified, values become a stabilising force. They guide you when choices are complex and help you align your goals with who you truly are. A goal that contradicts your values will always create inner tension, no matter how impressive it appears from the outside.

Self-knowledge also requires a clear view of your strengths and limitations. To recognise your strengths is not arrogance; it is self-respect. It allows you to direct your energy where it will be most effective. But equal honesty must be applied to understanding your limitations. This does not mean accepting weakness as permanent, but recognising where you need support, skill development, or a change in strategy. Growth begins where illusion ends. When you stop pretending that you can do everything, you begin to do the right things with focus and authenticity. Many people waste energy resisting their own nature, trying to become versions of themselves that fit external ideals. The paradox is that real transformation only becomes possible when you first accept yourself as you are. From acceptance comes clarity; from clarity, meaningful change.

To understand yourself fully, you must also examine the emotional patterns that shape your perception of life. Emotions are not irrational disturbances to be suppressed; they are forms of intelligence, providing insight into your needs and priorities. Anger may reveal where your boundaries have been crossed. Sadness may signal a loss that needs to be acknowledged. Anxiety may point toward areas of uncertainty requiring preparation. When you stop running from your emotions and begin to listen to them, they transform from obstacles into guides. This emotional literacy allows you to make decisions grounded in awareness rather than reaction.

Another essential dimension of self-understanding is your relationship with time and change. We often cling to past identities or outdated definitions of ourselves, mistaking consistency for integrity. But who you are is not static. It evolves as you encounter new experiences and gain new insight. To understand yourself is therefore an ongoing process, not a single conclusion. Each stage of life asks new questions and demands new answers. The goals that fit your twenty-year-old self may no longer serve your thirty-year-old self. The priorities of a student may differ from those of a parent, an entrepreneur, or a retiree. Growth means being willing to update your understanding of who you are without betraying your essence. It means allowing renewal to coexist with continuity.

Self-knowledge also includes the courage to question your own motives. We often present our actions as selfless, rational, or noble, but beneath the surface, subtler impulses operate: the need for validation, the fear of rejection, the desire for control. To acknowledge these hidden layers is not to condemn yourself but to become honest. Awareness does not weaken morality; it strengthens it by replacing pretence with sincerity. When you can look at yourself without defence, your choices become clearer, your relationships more authentic, and your goals more meaningful.

Reflection is the method through which understanding deepens. It can take many forms, journaling, conversation, meditation, or simply quiet thought at the end of the day. The form matters less than the attitude. Reflection is not an exercise in judgment, but in discernment. It asks, "What did I learn today about myself?" and listens without rushing to a conclusion. Over time, this habit builds inner clarity, allowing you to navigate challenges with less confusion. In moments of doubt, returning to reflection reconnects you to your own wisdom, reminding you that understanding is not something you find outside yourself, but something you cultivate within.

Understanding yourself also means recognising the environments that help or hinder your growth. Just as plants need the right soil, people thrive in the right settings, places that align with their temperament, energy, and values. Some individuals flourish in structure and predictability; others need freedom and exploration. Some draw energy from collaboration; others from solitude. The more honest you are about the conditions under which you do your best work, the easier it becomes to design a life that supports your nature rather than suppresses it. This self-knowledge is not indulgent; it is efficient. It ensures that your effort produces growth rather than resistance.

Ultimately, to understand yourself is to become your own ally. It is to stop fighting who you are and start working with yourself. When you know what inspires you, what drains you, what patterns repeat, and what truly matters, life becomes less about control and more about cooperation with your own inner nature. You begin to act with greater ease, because your choices are no longer scattered. Your outer world starts to reflect the quiet order you have built within. Goals become clearer, not because life has simplified, but because you have.

And perhaps the most profound discovery in all of this is that understanding yourself is not a destination, but a relationship, a lifelong conversation between who you are, who you have been, and who you are becoming. It requires patience, humility, and the willingness to change. Yet it rewards you with something rare and enduring: a sense of wholeness that no external success can replace. Once you know yourself, you no longer chase approval or perfection. You move through life with quiet conviction, aware that every challenge, every failure, every victory is simply another opportunity to see yourself more clearly. And in that clarity lies the freedom to live, to grow, and to become everything you were meant to be.

7

LEARNING THROUGH LIFE

Life itself is the greatest classroom you will ever enter. From the day you take your first breath, you are learning through every interaction, every mistake, every success, and every silence. Yet somewhere along the way, many people begin to separate learning from living. They start to believe that education ends with school or that knowledge belongs only to books and formal institutions. This false division between life and learning quietly drains curiosity and limits growth. The truth is that life never stops teaching. Each moment contains a lesson, waiting for attention. Every setback, every encounter, every fleeting joy is an invitation to understand something more deeply about yourself and the world. To learn through life means to remain open, to move through each day not with certainty but with curiosity, and to recognise that wisdom is gathered not by age or title but by awareness.

At its core, learning is an act of humility. It begins with the willingness to admit what you do not yet know and to see ignorance not as a flaw but as an opportunity. The humble learner listens before speaking, observes before judging, and asks before assuming. This mindset keeps the mind flexible and the heart alive. People who believe they already understand everything lose the ability to grow because their certainty blinds them. They stop noticing new details and start repeating old conclusions. Their lives become predictable patterns rather than evolving journeys. In contrast, those who remain curious approach every experience as a chance to see differently. They question even their own opinions and welcome correction because they know that growth often hides behind discomfort. A learning mind never ages; it stays young through its openness to wonder.

To live as a lifelong learner, you must expand your understanding of what learning actually means. Real education does not belong only to classrooms or exams; it also arises through living, observing, and reflecting. Books teach principles, but life teaches application. Challenges teach adaptability, failure teaches humility, and relationships teach empathy. Every difficulty you face can become a source of instruction if you pause long enough to ask what it is showing you. A difficult colleague may teach patience. A moment of rejection may strengthen resilience. Even boredom can reveal the parts of life you have neglected to explore. Learning, in its truest form, is not about collecting information. It is about integrating experience and using it to refine your understanding of who you are and what matters most.

Every person you meet can serve as a teacher, often without intending to. Some people teach you through wisdom, kindness, or guidance. Others teach you through challenge, conflict, or disappointment. The ones who frustrate you often reveal more about your own nature than the ones who comfort you. They expose your impatience, pride, or unexamined beliefs. When you begin to view people as mirrors rather than obstacles, every encounter gains meaning. A friend who offers advice, a stranger who shows kindness, a critic who provokes irritation, all of them reflect aspects of your own growth. If you can observe your reactions to them without defensiveness, you transform irritation into insight. You start to see that life is not punishing you with difficult people; it is polishing you through them.

Many of life's most powerful lessons emerge not from success but from disruption. When plans collapse, when losses strike, when the familiar disappears, you are forced to see differently. These moments of rupture tear open the layers of comfort that keep you from growing. The loss of a job may feel like failure, but it can become the beginning of reinvention. A broken relationship may leave pain, but it also teaches boundaries, communication, and the depth of your own capacity to heal. Pain, when faced honestly, becomes a teacher of clarity. It strips away illusion and reminds you of what cannot be taken away: your strength, your adaptability, and your will to continue. Growth rarely comes from what is easy. It comes from what challenges your sense of self and demands you evolve.

Learning through life also requires the ability to observe yourself with honesty. The mind that watches itself grows wiser with each passing day. Begin to notice your thoughts, habits, and emotional patterns. See how you respond to stress, how you make decisions, and how you treat others when you are tired or afraid. Observation without judgment is the foundation of insight. When you understand the mechanisms behind your behaviour, you gain freedom. You can pause before reacting, choose your words with awareness, and redirect your energy toward what truly matters. This kind of learning is deeper than academic study because it changes not only what you know but who you are.

Mistakes, too, play an essential role in learning. Many people grow up fearing failure as though it were proof of inadequacy. In truth, mistakes are evidence that you are trying, that you are experimenting with new possibilities. The greatest innovators, artists, and thinkers have all failed repeatedly before achieving anything lasting. Each failure clarified their method, sharpened their discipline, and taught them what does not work. The difference between those who succeed and those who stop lies not in intelligence but in interpretation. One person views failure as an ending, while another sees it as a message. The latter learns faster because they stay curious even in defeat. If you can learn to treat your mistakes as teachers rather than enemies, your progress becomes unstoppable.

To remain a lifelong learner, you must also allow yourself to be surprised. The most valuable discoveries often arrive unplanned. A conversation overheard, a book found by chance, or a simple walk in nature can reveal truths that years of study cannot. The secret is to stay attentive. When your life is filled with distraction and rush, you miss the quiet lessons hiding in ordinary moments. Try noticing small details, a colour, a sound, a smile, and you may find that the world has been teaching you all along. Serendipity is not luck but awareness meeting opportunity.

In the modern age, information is everywhere, but understanding is rare. Technology has made knowledge abundant and instantly available, but abundance is not the same as depth. Many people confuse information with wisdom, believing that exposure equals insight. Real learning does not happen through constant consumption but through deliberate reflection. Ask yourself what each new piece of information means to you. Does it change how you see yourself or others? Does it connect with your experience or values? When you take time to think, you transform information into understanding and understanding into wisdom. This slower, more conscious approach to learning protects your attention from becoming scattered and keeps your mind anchored in what truly matters.

Part of learning through life involves the difficult process of unlearning. As you grow, some beliefs, habits, and assumptions outlive their usefulness. The perspectives that once helped you survive or succeed can later become barriers. Unlearning means releasing what no longer serves you, even if it once felt essential. It requires courage because it often involves questioning long-held truths or identities. Yet this shedding is necessary for renewal. A tree cannot grow new leaves without letting go of the old. In the same way, you cannot evolve if you remain attached to outdated patterns. The act of unlearning clears space for new insight to take root.

Some of the most profound lessons life teaches arrive through pain. Loss, illness, and failure do not merely test endurance; they expand understanding. They teach empathy for others and compassion for yourself. They show you how to sit with uncertainty, how to accept imperfection, and how to find meaning even in suffering. These lessons are not sought, but when embraced, they become transformative. They remind you that knowledge is not just the mastery of facts but the maturity of the soul. The person who learns through pain often emerges more patient, more open, and more aware of life's fragility.

Ultimately, learning through life is not a project that ever ends. There is no finish line, no final achievement that marks completion. Learning continues as long as you are alive and paying attention. What changes is not the presence of lessons, but your ability to recognise them. With time, you begin to see connections between experiences that once seemed unrelated. You realise that life is not a series of separate events but a continuous conversation between who you are and who you are becoming. The teacher and the student live within the same person.

To learn through life is to live awake. It means moving through your days with awareness rather than routine, seeing every experience as meaningful, and remaining humble enough to learn even when you think you know. It means being curious about the world and about yourself, seeking growth not as a duty but as a way of honouring the time you have. When you live in this way, wisdom ceases to be something far away. It becomes the natural byproduct of a life lived attentively. Learning through life is not about perfection but about depth, not about mastery but about understanding. It teaches you not only how to succeed, but how to see, how to listen, and how to live fully in the ever-changing classroom of existence.

ஐ

8

WORKING WITH OTHERS

No one achieves anything of lasting value alone. Every goal, no matter how personal, is touched in some way by others, through inspiration, support, challenge, or cooperation. To work with others is not only to share tasks, but to engage in one of life's most complex and rewarding forms of learning. Human relationships form the network through which ideas move, decisions are made, and meaning is created. Whether in friendships, study groups, professional teams, or families, the ability to work well with others determines not only your success but also the quality of your daily experience. Collaboration is not simply about efficiency. It is about expanding what is possible by joining strengths, perspectives, and energies that no individual could fully embody alone.

Working with others begins with understanding that collaboration is an exchange, not a contest. It requires seeing people as partners rather than competitors, as individuals with different gifts rather than threats to your own. This mindset shift is foundational. When you approach others with curiosity and respect instead of comparison, you create an atmosphere where cooperation can thrive. People are more willing to share ideas when they feel seen and valued. Conversely, environments driven by ego or insecurity often produce silence and resistance. True teamwork is built on trust, and trust grows where there is sincerity. The most effective collaborators are those who listen as intently as they speak, who care about understanding before being understood, and who focus on shared outcomes rather than personal recognition.

At its best, collaboration brings together diverse minds to solve problems that no one could manage alone. Each person brings a different set of strengths, analytical, creative, emotional, or strategic. The power lies in learning how to blend these abilities rather than flatten them into sameness. Consider a project where one person excels at detail and another at vision. If both insist that their way is right, the group fractures. But if each respects the other's difference, detail gives structure to vision and vision gives meaning to detail. This complementarity turns diversity into power. It is a reminder that the goal of working with others is not agreement, but alignment. An agreement may produce harmony, but alignment moves.

Communication is the core skill that makes collaboration possible. Clear, honest, and empathetic communication bridges the gap between different perspectives. It allows misunderstandings to be addressed before they grow into conflict. Good communication is not simply speaking well; it is the art of conveying what matters in a way others can receive. It means expressing expectations clearly, asking for feedback openly, and listening with the intent to understand rather than to respond. Many conflicts that appear personal are actually problems of unclear communication. Learning to clarify your thoughts, to check assumptions, and to ask better questions can transform how smoothly a group functions. A team that communicates effectively moves like a single organism, responding fluidly to challenges and changes.

Yet working with others also demands patience, because people differ not only in skill but in temperament, rhythm, and background. What energises one person may drain another. What feels urgent to you may seem trivial to someone else. Recognising these differences without judgment allows for balance. In a healthy team, each person's nature is acknowledged and used wisely. The extrovert's enthusiasm fuels momentum; the introvert's reflection brings depth. The organiser ensures order; the dreamer keeps the vision alive. When everyone is allowed to contribute authentically, the team grows more resilient. Cooperation then becomes not a compromise but a shared art, where differences are tuned into harmony.

Conflict, though uncomfortable, is an inevitable part of working with others. It is not a sign that something has gone wrong, but that something important is being negotiated. The goal is not to avoid conflict, but to handle it constructively. When disagreement arises, pause before reacting. Ask what value or need is being protected by each side. Often, beneath every argument lies a legitimate concern, a desire for respect, for autonomy, for clarity, or for fairness. When you address these underlying needs rather than only the surface issue, resolution becomes possible. Constructive conflict sharpens understanding, strengthens relationships, and leads to better decisions. It teaches empathy, reminding you that collaboration requires courage as much as cooperation.

One of the most underestimated skills in working with others is the ability to give and receive feedback. Many people either avoid it altogether or deliver it in ways that wound rather than help. Yet thoughtful feedback is essential for growth. It acts as a mirror, showing you aspects of your performance you cannot see alone. When giving feedback, focus on behaviour rather than character. Describe what you observed and how it affected the work, then invite dialogue rather than dictating a verdict. When receiving feedback, resist the instinct to defend yourself immediately. Listen, reflect, and decide what is useful. You do not have to agree with everything you hear, but the willingness to consider another perspective keeps you adaptable. Over time, this openness transforms feedback from a threat into a gift.

Trust is the invisible thread that holds collaboration together. It cannot be demanded; it must be earned through consistency, integrity, and transparency. You build trust by keeping your word, by admitting mistakes instead of hiding them, and by recognising the contributions of others. Small gestures, meeting deadlines, following through on promises, and giving credit generously accumulate into reliability. Once trust is established, communication becomes easier, creativity flows more freely, and collective effort feels natural. Without trust, even the most talented group struggles, because energy is wasted on protection instead of progress.

Working with others also teaches humility. You quickly realise that you are not the centre of every process, that others see things you cannot, and that success often depends on contributions you do not fully control. This realisation can be humbling, but it is also freeing. It shifts your focus from self-importance to shared purpose. When you stop needing to prove yourself in every interaction, you make room for genuine collaboration. You begin to appreciate not only what others do, but who they are. The act of working together becomes less about efficiency and more about humanity.

In modern life, collaboration extends beyond physical spaces. Digital tools, remote work, and global networks have made teamwork more flexible but also more complex. Virtual collaboration demands heightened clarity and intentionality. Without the subtle cues of body language, words carry greater weight. In such settings, written communication must be precise, and empathy must be expressed consciously. When distance separates people, regular check-ins, shared goals, and transparent communication help maintain connection. The principles remain the same: trust, respect, and understanding, but the mediums require adaptation. Technology should serve collaboration, not replace it.

The deeper purpose of working with others lies not only in shared achievement but in personal growth. Collaboration reveals your own tendencies, how you handle responsibility, how you respond to pressure, and how you treat people when outcomes are uncertain. It shows you your capacity for patience, generosity, and compromise. These qualities, once cultivated, extend far beyond the workplace. They improve relationships, strengthen communities, and enrich the inner life. To work well with others is, in essence, to live well among others. It is to participate consciously in the web of connection that sustains all human progress.

At its highest level, collaboration becomes a form of collective intelligence. When individuals contribute freely, guided by trust and shared vision, the group begins to think as one. Ideas evolve faster, creativity multiplies, and solutions emerge that no single mind could have produced. This is the quiet magic of working together: the creation of something larger than any individual, something that carries the imprint of many minds yet belongs to none.

Ultimately, learning to work with others is a lifelong discipline. It requires self-awareness, emotional maturity, and the ability to balance your individuality with the needs of the collective. It asks you to listen deeply, speak truthfully, and act generously. When you master these qualities, collaboration ceases to feel like an obligation. It becomes a privilege, a way of expanding your humanity by connecting it to others. The people you work with become not just companions in projects, but fellow travellers in the shared journey of becoming. Together, you build not only success but meaning, not only results but relationships, and through that process, you learn one of life's most important lessons: that we rise higher when we rise together.

ꟼꝹ

9

TOOLS FOR PROGRESS

Progress does not happen by accident. It is shaped by the tools you choose, the structures you build, and the habits you sustain. Every goal, no matter how inspired, must pass through the discipline of execution, through the quiet daily rhythm that turns vision into reality. In these moments, tools serve as bridges between intention and achievement. They transform vague ambition into measurable momentum. But the best tools are not always external. They include your mindset, your capacity for reflection, and your ability to convert knowledge into consistent action. When you learn to use both the tools outside you and those within, progress becomes less about pressure and more about direction.

The most essential tool is clarity. Clarity acts as both a compass and a foundation. It filters noise, simplifies choices, and gives shape to your energy. Without clarity, effort diffuses, and you end up working hard in circles. To find clarity, pause and define your "why." Why is this goal important? What will it change in your life? What values does it express? Many people chase goals that belong more to social expectation than personal conviction, and the result is exhaustion without fulfilment. Write your reasons in detail, not as slogans but as honest answers. When clarity is strong, even difficult work feels meaningful.

Once clarity is in place, structure becomes your next ally. Structure gives rhythm to purpose. It is the framework that helps you balance intention with discipline. Structure can take many forms, such as a daily schedule, a calendar reminder, or a consistent morning ritual. For example, a writer might decide that every morning between six and eight is sacred writing time, no matter the weather or mood. A student might allocate one hour each evening to review and summarise lessons before sleep. These small, predictable anchors are what carry you through moments of distraction. Structure should never feel like confinement. When well-designed, it feels like support, a quiet scaffolding that keeps your focus steady even when motivation wavers.

Another indispensable tool is reflection. Without reflection, even efficient routines can become mechanical. Reflection helps you distinguish movement from progress and activity from growth. Set aside regular time to pause and evaluate. You can do this weekly, monthly, or at the end of each project. Ask yourself simple but powerful questions: What worked? What did not? What can I improve? Record your thoughts in a journal or voice note. Over time, these records become a personal archive of your learning, proof that you have evolved not only in output but in understanding. Reflection is how you turn experience into wisdom.

In the age of digital abundance, countless productivity systems promise transformation: planners, apps, bullet journals, digital boards, time trackers. But the best tool is the one you actually use consistently. You do not need a perfect method; you need a rhythm that fits your nature. Try what appeals to you, but stop searching for the next new system once you find something that feels natural. Too much optimisation becomes procrastination in disguise. For some, a notebook and pen work better than any app. For others, digital dashboards create the structure they need. What matters is not how advanced the tool looks, but whether it deepens your awareness and sustains your effort.

Among all external tools, habit is the most powerful internal one. Habits turn effort into instinct. When you repeat an action often enough, it begins to run on its own momentum, freeing your energy for creativity. To build a habit, start small. If your goal is to read daily, begin with ten pages, not fifty. If you aim to meditate, start with two minutes of breathing, not half an hour of stillness. Attach the habit to an existing anchor such as reading after breakfast, reflecting before bed, or exercising before your morning shower. Consistency, not intensity, creates change. The first few weeks are the hardest because your brain resists new patterns, but repetition rewires it. Over time, the action feels natural, even incomplete without it. That is how habits become invisible engines of growth.

Technology, when guided by awareness, can become an extraordinary ally. A digital calendar can help you visualise commitments and reduce mental clutter. A note-taking app can capture fleeting ideas before they vanish. Even simple tools like a timer can transform productivity. The Pomodoro technique, for instance, alternates twenty-five minutes of focused work with five minutes of rest, making large tasks less intimidating. However, the same tools can become traps when used without discipline. Constant notifications, multiple overlapping apps, and endless productivity tweaks can drain focus. Periodically audit your digital tools. Ask yourself whether they simplify your life or complicate it. Use technology consciously, not compulsively.

Accountability is another quiet but powerful tool. It connects your private intentions to the shared world of commitment. When you declare a goal aloud to a friend, mentor, or partner, you convert it from possibility into promise. Accountability creates gentle pressure and shared encouragement. You can design it formally through mastermind groups or mentorship check-ins, or informally by discussing your weekly goals with someone you trust. Over time, this external accountability transforms into internal integrity. You no longer need others to keep you on track; your sense of honesty with yourself becomes enough.

Another subtle yet indispensable tool is patience. In the race for progress, patience is often mistaken for passivity, but it is actually the ultimate expression of confidence. Progress unfolds unevenly. There are days when growth feels visible and others when it hides beneath repetition. Patience allows you to trust the process even when results are not immediate. It teaches you to value process over pace, to see each step as meaningful, and to trust that consistent effort compounds quietly. When you cultivate patience, frustration turns into endurance, and endurance turns into mastery.

One practical exercise that combines several of these tools is what you might call the Monthly Progress Audit. At the end of each month, take an hour for yourself. Review your notes, your tasks, your reflections, and your results. Divide a page into three sections: Continue, Adjust, and Release. In the first, note what is working and bringing value. In the second, record what feels misaligned or draining. In the third, list what you no longer need to pursue. This ritual prevents stagnation, helps you realign priorities, and keeps your path flexible. It reminds you that tools exist to serve your growth, not the other way around.

The most overlooked tool of all is joy. Joy is not merely pleasure; it is the quiet satisfaction of meaningful effort. When you enjoy the process, when you find small moments of fulfilment in practice, collaboration, or progress, consistency stops feeling like duty. Joy keeps the heart engaged when discipline begins to tire. Cultivate it by choosing methods that feel natural, by celebrating small wins, and by working in spaces that inspire calm or curiosity. Joy renews energy faster than rest. It is the most sustainable fuel for progress.

Ultimately, tools are only as powerful as the awareness with which you use them. They are not ends in themselves but extensions of attention. A tool used mindlessly becomes a distraction. A tool used consciously becomes a channel for purpose. The goal is to design a life where your tools, whether mental, physical, or digital, work together like a quiet orchestra. Each plays a role in maintaining balance, clarity, and flow. When your tools align with your values, effort becomes elegant. You stop pushing your life forward and begin guiding it. Progress becomes less about speed and more about coherence, a steady unfolding of what is possible when intention and structure move in harmony.

☙❧

10

SELF-ANALYSIS

Learning to Study Yourself

Studying yourself is one of the most profound investments you can make. The ability to observe your thoughts, reactions, and patterns with honesty is what separates direction from drift. Most people spend their lives studying the world around them, jobs, systems, technologies, and other people, yet rarely stop to understand the one mind through which all experience is filtered. Without self-knowledge, even the best strategies can misfire. You may chase goals that look appealing but fail to satisfy, work tirelessly but feel unfulfilled, or repeat the same obstacles without knowing why. Self-analysis is not about self-criticism. It is about awareness. It means becoming both student and teacher of your own life.

The first step in studying yourself is learning to observe rather than react. Each day offers opportunities to notice how you think, how you decide, and what triggers your emotions. Pay attention to recurring patterns, the habits that return whenever you are stressed or uncertain. Do you avoid certain tasks until the last minute? Do you overcommit to please others and then feel drained? Do you lose motivation when results are slow? These small observations reveal the invisible scripts that guide your actions. Awareness of them is the beginning of freedom. When you name a pattern, you take away its power to control you.

Another essential aspect of self-analysis is reflection on values. Many of our decisions are guided by values we inherit rather than choose. Take time to examine what principles genuinely guide you. What do you consider non-negotiable in your life? Integrity, freedom, compassion, growth, stability, your values form the moral architecture of your choices. When your goals align with your values, effort feels meaningful. When they conflict, even success feels hollow. For example, someone who values creativity may feel trapped in a highly structured job, while another who values security may find a volatile entrepreneurial life draining. By identifying what you truly stand for, you gain a compass that helps you make choices with consistency and peace.

To deepen self-understanding, it helps to ask questions that go beneath the surface. Try reflecting on a few key areas: What gives me energy, and what drains it? What situations make me defensive or anxious? What do I fear losing the most? What kind of praise matters most to me, and why? These questions are not meant to produce instant answers but to start a process of insight. The goal is not to fix yourself but to understand yourself. The more honest your answers, the more clearly you will see how your emotions, beliefs, and ambitions interact.

Journaling is one of the most effective tools for self-analysis. It is not about recording daily events but about capturing inner weather, your moods, decisions, doubts, and insights. Write without judgment or concern for structure. Describe how you felt during the day, what you avoided, what you enjoyed, and what you learned. Over time, patterns will emerge naturally. You will see which triggers lead to procrastination, which routines increase focus, and which people energise or drain you. This record becomes a mirror you can consult whenever confusion returns. In a world that moves quickly, journaling slows your thoughts just enough to see them clearly.

Self-analysis also requires understanding your strengths and weaknesses without distortion. Many people either overestimate their abilities or underestimate them entirely. Both extremes are barriers to growth. Try to take an objective view of yourself. What are you naturally good at? What skills feel intuitive and rewarding? Conversely, what tasks leave you frustrated or resistant? Recognising these patterns does not mean resigning yourself to them. It means working intelligently. A person who knows they are easily distracted can design an environment that limits interruptions. Someone who struggles with self-discipline can build accountability through partnerships or tracking systems. When you know your tendencies, you can design around them rather than constantly fighting against them.

Emotional awareness is another vital layer of self-study. Emotions are not distractions from rational thinking; they are information about your needs, fears, and values. Learning to read them accurately turns emotion into intelligence. Notice the emotion behind your actions. Are you working late because you are inspired, or because you are afraid of falling behind? Are you saying yes to commitments out of generosity, or out of fear of disapproval? The reason matters because intention shapes experience. The more you align your actions with authentic emotion rather than fear or habit, the more coherent your life becomes.

You can also study yourself through your reactions to others. Relationships are mirrors that reflect what you believe about yourself. The people who irritate or intimidate you often reveal unresolved parts of your own character. For instance, if someone's confidence annoys you, it may be pointing toward a confidence you have not yet owned. Instead of judging, use these reactions as data. Ask yourself what they reveal about your own insecurities or aspirations. Over time, this practice dissolves blame and strengthens empathy, because you begin to see that what frustrates you in others often lives quietly within you.

Self-analysis does not mean constant introspection to the point of paralysis. The goal is awareness followed by action. Once you identify a pattern, take a small step toward changing it. If you tend to avoid uncomfortable conversations, schedule one and prepare for it thoughtfully. If you often feel unfocused, adjust your workspace and block time for deep work. Insight becomes valuable only when translated into behaviour. Every moment of awareness should eventually lead to movement, even if small.

One practical exercise is the Weekly Review. At the end of each week, take fifteen minutes to answer three questions: What did I learn about myself this week? Where did I act in alignment with my values, and where did I drift? What is one adjustment I can make next week? Keep these notes together in a single notebook. Reading them back after a few months will reveal progress you may not have noticed, shifts in awareness, language, and energy that accumulate quietly but meaningfully.

Another way to strengthen self-knowledge is through feedback. Others can often see patterns we overlook. Ask a few trusted people to describe your strengths and your blind spots. Listen without defending.

Feedback is not a verdict; it is information. If something resonates, reflect on it. If it does not, let it go. The purpose of feedback is not to please others but to see yourself more clearly.

As you deepen this process, it becomes clear that self-analysis is not a one-time exercise but a lifelong dialogue with yourself. Who you are changes with experience, and so does what you need to learn. There will be seasons of confusion, clarity, and renewal. The key is to remain curious about your own evolution. Growth is not always visible, but awareness itself is a form of progress.

Self-analysis ultimately leads to self-trust. When you understand how you think and why you act, you stop relying entirely on external validation. You begin to trust your judgment and decisions because they are rooted in self-awareness rather than impulse. This inner confidence creates stability even in uncertainty. You may not always know the outcome, but you know how to respond. That knowledge is one of life's greatest forms of freedom.

Finally, remember that understanding yourself is not about reaching perfection. It is about becoming more conscious, more intentional, and more compassionate toward the person you already are. When you study yourself with kindness, awareness becomes transformation. You begin to notice how every challenge, mistake, and breakthrough has shaped you. The more clearly you see yourself, the better equipped you are to set goals that truly reflect your essence. And when your goals emerge from genuine understanding, progress becomes not just achievement, but self-expression.

ஐ

CONCLUSION

Living the Realisation

To set goals is to shape time with intention. It is the act of taking the abstract flow of days and giving it direction, meaning, and form. It is an acknowledgement that life, though uncertain, can be guided by purpose. To pursue a goal is to participate consciously in your own becoming. It means deciding that you will not drift wherever the current takes you, but will instead chart a course that reflects who you are and what you value most deeply. To realise your goals, however, is not just about success in the conventional sense. It is about living with awareness, acting with clarity, and allowing your choices to express the person you wish to be.

Throughout this journey, you have explored many aspects of what it means to live with purpose. You have examined how goals give structure to life and how purpose gives those goals meaning. You have learned how planning bridges the space between thought and action, and how motivation and willpower fuel consistency. You have also seen that understanding yourself, your values, and your inner drives determines the quality of your efforts more than any technique or system. All of these are not isolated lessons but interconnected layers of one truth: growth begins with awareness and endures through deliberate action.

The process of goal realisation is not a straight path. It moves through cycles of clarity and confusion, effort and rest, progress and pause. At times, you will feel unstoppable, and at other times, you will doubt your capacity to continue. These moments of uncertainty are not signs of weakness. They are part of the rhythm of growth. Every journey includes seasons of acceleration and seasons of stillness. The stillness is not wasted time. It is the soil in which new insights take root. When you allow yourself to pause, reflect, and realign, you return to your goals not only with renewed energy but with a greater understanding of why they matter.

True fulfilment does not come from crossing every goal off your list but from knowing that what you pursue reflects your truth. When your goals align with your values, even the hard days feel worthwhile. You may face resistance, obstacles, or failure, but these moments are opportunities to strengthen your inner clarity. They teach patience, humility, and resilience. They remind you that real growth is not measured by how quickly you reach an endpoint, but by how consciously you engage with the process itself. Every challenge overcome, every lesson learned, adds to the foundation of who you are becoming.

In a world that often glorifies busyness, it is easy to mistake constant activity for progress. But true progress is quieter. It is found in the intention behind your actions, in the quality of your focus, and in your ability to remain steady even when results are not immediate.

The person who learns to value the process will always move further than the one who seeks only results. The act of working toward something meaningful changes you from within. It cultivates depth, maturity, and grace. It teaches you that patience and perseverance are not weaknesses but strengths that carry you through uncertainty with dignity.

Over time, you may discover that your goals evolve. The ambitions that once guided you might lose their pull, while new desires begin to take shape. This is not an inconsistency. It is the natural rhythm of an expanding life. As you grow, your understanding of what truly matters becomes more refined. Do not cling to old goals out of habit or fear of change. Allow yourself to evolve. Redefining your goals is not a step backwards but an act of courage, an acknowledgement that self-awareness always deepens with time. The goals you set today are not final destinations but expressions of your current understanding of who you are.

Remember that reflection is an essential part of this process. Reflection turns experience into wisdom. It allows you to look back not with regret but with gratitude for what each step has taught you. Make it a practice to pause regularly and ask yourself: What did I learn? How have I changed? What still matters, and what no longer does? These questions bring you closer to clarity and keep your life aligned with your evolving purpose. When you reflect, you reclaim ownership of your story.

Equally important is compassion, both for yourself and for others. The pursuit of goals can sometimes make you rigid or self-critical, especially when progress feels slow. But remember that you are not a machine built to perform; you are a human being learning to grow. Treat yourself with patience. Celebrate the small victories and learn gently from your mistakes. Compassion does not mean complacency. It means recognising that growth is imperfect and that imperfection itself is part of what makes it meaningful.

The more you live with awareness, the more you begin to see that realisation is not an endpoint but a state of being. It is not something you reach once and then possess forever. It is something you live, moment by moment, through the way you make decisions, the way you respond to challenges, and the way you honour your values in daily life. To realise your goals is to embody them, to let your actions become an expression of your intentions. It is about learning to walk in harmony with your purpose, not racing toward it.

At its deepest level, goal realisation is about integrity. It is about making your outer life reflect your inner truth. When what you think, what you feel, and what you do all align, you experience a sense of peace that no external achievement can replace. That peace becomes your compass, guiding you through uncertainty and distraction. With integrity, even the smallest task becomes meaningful, because it is performed with awareness and care.

If there is one lesson to carry with you beyond these pages, it is this: you already possess what you need to begin. The tools, the strength, the creativity, and the resilience are within you. They may be hidden beneath doubt or habit, but they are there, waiting to be awakened through action. You do not need perfect conditions to start. You need only the willingness to take one deliberate step, to reflect on what you learn, and to take the next. With each step, clarity grows stronger and confidence follows naturally.

So begin where you are. Set your goals, refine them, and stay close to your purpose. When you stumble, pause and learn. When you succeed, pause and be grateful. Allow every phase of your journey to teach you something about who you are and what you are capable of. The destination will take care of itself if you walk with awareness, patience, and sincerity.

In the end, goal realisation is not about achieving more. It is about living more fully. It is about waking each day with intention and going to bed with the quiet satisfaction of having acted in alignment with what truly matters. It is about becoming the kind of person whose life, in every small and large way, expresses their purpose. To live this way is to live consciously, to live freely, and to live well.

And perhaps, after all this reflection and effort, you will come to understand that the most meaningful words in your journey are not "I wish" or "I will" but "I am." When you live with purpose, you are already realising your goals with every thought, every action, and every moment that you choose to live with awareness and care.

ജ്ഞ